Ghosts of the Tower of London

Ghosts of the Tower of London

G. ABBOTT

Yeoman Warder (retd)
HM Tower of London
Member of Her Majesty's Bodyguard of the
Yeomen of the Guard Extraordinary

Verses by Shelagh Abbott

HENDON PUBLISHING : NELSON

Published by William Heinemann Ltd 1980
Reprinted 1980 (twice), 1982
Published by David & Charles 1986
Published by
Hendon Publishing Co. Ltd.
1989
Reprinted 1992

ISBN 0 86067 123 2

Printed in England by The Amadeus Press Ltd., Huddersfield
for
Hendon Publishing Co. Ltd., Hendon Mill,
Nelson, Lancashire

Contents

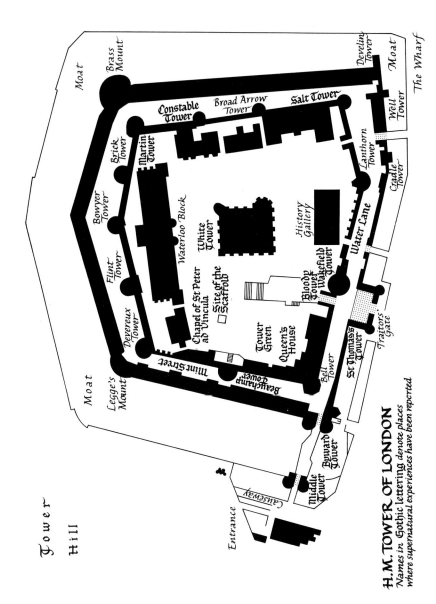

Tower Hill

Moat

Moat

Brass Mount

Constable Tower

Broad Arrow Tower

Salt Tower

Develin Tower

Moat

The Wharf

Well Tower

Brick Tower

Martin Tower

Lanthorn Tower

Cradle Tower

Bowyer Tower

Waterloo Block

White Tower

History Gallery

Flint Tower

Chapel of St Peter ad Vincula

Site of the Scaffold

Wakefield Tower

Water Lane

Devereux Tower

Bloody Tower

Legge's Mount

Mint Street

Tower Green

Queen's House

St Thomas's Tower

Traitors' Gate

Beauchamp Tower

Bell Tower

Byward Tower

Causeway

Middle Tower

Entrance

H.M. TOWER OF LONDON
Names in Gothic lettering denote places where supernatural experiences have been reported

Foreword

Ghost stories have a certain fascination for most people, whether or not they believe in them, and it is difficult to imagine a more appropriate habitation for ghosts (if they exist) than Her Majesty's Tower of London, with its nine hundred years of eventful and, at times, grim and violent history.

Over the centuries, and indeed in recent times, people have reported inexplicable sights and sounds in the Tower. Yeoman Warder Abbott is to be congratulated on his carefully researched collection of these experiences, made additionally interesting by the inclusion of historic details of the Tower and of the victims whose ghosts are said to haunt their erstwhile prison.

I am confident that the reader will find this little book both interesting and instructive.

Field Marshal Sir Geoffrey Baker
GCB CMG CBE MC
Constable of Her Majesty's
Tower of London

October 1979

Acknowledgements

Grateful acknowledgements to the Constable of Her Majesty's Tower of London, Field Marshal Sir Geoffrey Baker, GCB, CMG, CBE, MC, the Resident Governor 1971–79, Major General Sir W. D. M. Raeburn, KCVO, CB, DSO, MBE, MA, and to his successor, Major General Giles Mills, CB, OBE. Also those of my colleagues, past and present, without whose experiences this book would have been a spiritless effort indeed!

The verses at the beginning of each section were written especially for this little book by my wife Shelagh, to whom I am deeply grateful both for them and for so much besides.

DEDICATED
TO MY COLLEAGUES
THE YEOMAN WARDERS
OF
HER MAJESTY'S TOWER OF
LONDON

When the merry wag doth hush his voice
And cower . . . then shall ye know
That ghosts do walk within this ancient Tower.
Fact or fantasy, truth or tale,
As shadows shorten and the skies grow pale,
Can ye with certainty stand and claim
That voices called – but no man came?

Shelagh Abbott

Introduction

Be it summer or winter, daily the public pour in their thousands to Her Majesty's Tower of London. Jostling across the causeways over the moat they surge through the archways, their bright clothes contrasting with the grey walls, their incessant chatter penetrating the remotest cells of the prison towers. They bring their own holiday atmosphere with them as they swarm across Tower Green. Here a crowd listens enthralled to a yeoman warder, their 'Beefeater' guide, or stands impressed by the impassive sentry. Yonder the babel of many tongues echoes from the Jewel House approaches as the queue ebbs and flows. Coach parties noisily follow their hurrying leaders, children dash in vain to catch the perambulating pigeon – the scene is alive, a whirlpool of colour, of chatter and happy activity.

Yet when the last tourist is shepherded out beneath the Byward archway and the shadows start to lengthen across Tower Green, it almost seems as if the grey stone buildings shake off the traces of the day's artifi-

1

ciality. For night is the time for memories, and the Tower of London has indeed a surfeit of those. Happy ones, yes, of banquets and coronations, processions and merrymaking. But when the clouds scud across the moon and the wind sighs through the arrow slits, the fortress wraps its cloak of brooding isolation around itself, like an old enshawled woman staring into the embers. It is then that the evil memories of the past jostle to emerge.

Many have experienced the horror of those memories. A ghostly figure flits across the Green; footsteps ascend stairs untrodden by human feet; a luminescent cylinder hovers above a table; huge shadows of terrifying shapes appear on battlemented walls. Memories conjuring up the countless wretches who suffered the agony of thumbscrew and rack, who perished beneath the axe. Could they not return, to reproach and bewail?

This book gathers together some of the reports of apparitions seen, inexplicable noises heard. That there have been more, I do not doubt. Not everyone is brave enough to admit fear, the bloodchilling terror which turns one's feet to stone, when one's twentieth-century brain refuses to accept the sight, the sound, the sensation of . . . who knows?

I do not seek to explain them, nor even to comment on the truth of their ever happening. You may laugh when the sun is high over the turrets, giggle with your friends as you ascend the spiral stairs in the Bloody Tower – sneer if you must as you crowd round the scaffold site.

But when the midnight mists wreathe low to shroud

the battlements – when the dark cavities of turret windows watch sardonically like half-closed eyes – when the wind, leaning gently on the oaken doors, causes pendant chains to swing and clank ... scoff not, but speed your stride and look not back!

Her Majesty's Royal Palace and Fortress, The Tower of London

In centuries to come shall it be said
Of this the Tower of London. . . .
Here stands a Keep that's kept its honest Word,
So Knights-defendant, helmet'd and spur'd,
Enharbour'd round by talismanic Bird,
May hold the Crown of England cherishèd.

No lesser structure could with honour claim
The nomen, Tower of London.
Though fastnesses abound this Island o'er,
Signals of feuding fashions, e'en of war,
Could there be none portraying Britain more,
To clarion her Fame.

Come then who may and brave the Dragon's mouth,
This tutelary Tower of London.
Arm ye with Halberd, Pike and Partizan,
Brandish and shout, ye Pinprick of a Man,
Our Nation's might shall live while still doth stand
This Panoply of Power in England's south.

5

The Tower of London by night

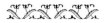

Dwarfed by the twentieth-century concrete blocks soaring above it, the Tower of London resembles a boy's toy fort left out on the lawn. Modern progress has stepped over it – none too deftly – and has strode on, the pace going faster and faster, the buildings of the City going higher and higher. Inventions have become more and more mind-bending and with each Space Age miracle people are more sophisticated. Yesterday's discoveries are taken for granted; last week's are forgotten.

Yet the veneer of civilization is thin. Even in this day and age the mention of 'going to the Tower' creates an unease in the mind, a faint whiff of apprehension that can only be dispelled by a joking allusion to the Axe, or a hope of an early reprieve! Why is this? Can it be that some primitive instinct of self-preservation has lingered through the centuries, some kind of horrific reminder of the terror that for many *was* the Tower?

Forget the high-rise blocks and monolithic hotels; return to the time when the houses of London were a mere six or seven feet high, made of wood, thatched with straw, huddled within the Roman Wall. But even that afforded little protection. First the Saxons and

7

Danes, at length the Normans came, triumphed and stayed. William the Conqueror needed a strong, secure residence in his capital, needed to defend the City from other attackers – needed also to control and subdue a sullen populace unwilling to accept its new overlord.

So with the Roman riverside wall to protect his southern flank and the landward wall guarding him against attack from the east, he built the central keep, the White Tower. Its height dominated the conquered City, its menacing defences were the symbol of its new master. Later two concentric walls surrounded it, with sturdy watchtowers at intervals along their lengths. A deep wide moat sustained by the river lapped around the outer wall, whilst drawbridges and heavily armed barbicans guarded its approaches. The fortress was complete.

So secure its strength, so impenetrable its walls, that the Tower, the first castle of its kind in Britain, became the very bastion of this country's destiny. For nearly six hundred years the Royal Families lived there. Remember that the man who had the Tower had the Power, for within its defences was stored the nation's chief armoury, sufficient to equip thousands of troops. The royal court presided there, advising on – or complying with – the monarch's decisions. The king's courts of justice had their sessions in the Inner Ward; the state treaties and papers were also held safe there. And because no king or queen could maintain power or finance wars or allies without gold, the Royal Mint operated within its walls, converting bullion into coinage. The State Regalia and Crown Jewels, as well as being symbolic of sovereignty, were items of immense value, and they too were safeguarded in this impregnable fortress.

To afford the Royal Family some recreation a menagerie was founded, the first 'zoo' in the land; science was advanced by establishing the Royal Observatory in the highest turret of the White Tower.

All monarchs had rivals, threats to their supremacy. Plotting barons and lords, defiant churchmen; even captured enemies holding promise of fat ransoms. Foolhardy indeed to imprison them away in the country, with the risk of their supporters achieving their escape – and so, as the depth of the moat and the height of the walls of the Tower of London could keep *out* the enemies of the State, they could equally keep *in* enemies of the State, making it also a State prison! It was not for the ordinary criminals of the day, the robbers, highwaymen, cutpurses and footpads. Such common miscreants had their own prisons out in London, and they met their end swinging from the end of a hempen rope.

The Tower of London's clientele were mainly aristocrats and high-ranking clergy accused of treason or heresy. The dreaded phrase 'committed to the Tower' meant at best a living death, some being incarcerated for up to fifteen years before sentence was carried out. At worst it resulted in public execution by the axe, or even being hanged, drawn and quartered. This latter involved semi-strangulation, disembowelling and virtual butchering. Should prisoners refuse to reveal the names of accomplices, they were subjected to fearsome torturing, which rarely failed.

As already stated, prisoners captured in battle were

lodged within the Tower, particularly those for whom a ransom could be demanded. John, King of Scots, was a captive in 1296; King David of Scotland was held for £100,000 in 1346; King John of France and his son, in 1361, were imprisoned in the Tower until 3,000,000 gold crowns were paid, while Charles, Duke of Orleans spent twenty-five years there until his countrymen could raise the 300,000 crowns demanded.

The Tower of London, then, played a major rôle in the evolution of the country's history. On occasions when it was necessary for the monarch to leave the Tower it was vital that during his absence it should be securely held by one absolutely loyal, one who would not betray his king by handing over his power base to rival factions.

This task of supreme importance was carried out by the Constable of the Tower of London. He was also known at different times as the Constable of London, Constable of the Sea and Constable of the Honour of London. He was – and is – one of the very few officials who have right of direct access to the Sovereign. In the Middle Ages he had many perquisites to augment his pay, not the least being extracted unwillingly from the prisoners – as did his second in command, the Lieutenant of the Tower.

Since 1685 the official actively in charge of the fortress has been the Major of the Tower, the present title being the Major and Resident Governor and Keeper of the Jewel House. Two Deputy governors assist him, and he also commands the Body of Yeoman Warders (the latter occasionally suffering the nickname of

Beefeaters!). This historic band of men, with their Chief Warder and Yeoman Gaoler, have been custodians of Her Majesty's Tower of London since the castle was built. Traditionally the guardians of the Crown Jewels at Coronations, they were also entrusted with keeping vigilant watch on the state prisoners. They were, and still are, members of the Royal Bodyguard. To those roles has also been added that of being a cicerone: a guide who learns and recounts the enthralling history of the Tower of London.

The Tower, then, far from being a defunct pile of stones is very much a living symbol of our historic past. Many of the original buildings remain; the State Regalia is on display, together with armour, weapons, even the execution axe, block and instruments of torture.

But is it only the tangible things that have survived? What of the wretches who suffered in the prison towers; have they really vanished into the limbo of the past? Or are they ever present, to reappear when least expected?

And will *you* be the next one to see them?

Execution on Tower Hill – Lord Lovat, 1747

The Threshold of the Tower of London

Lift thine head,
If thou hast yet the gut and will,
Ere Black Cap lifts it for you,
Leaving thy corpse to rest as still
As all the crowd around.
Lift thine head and look aloft for strength,
Before thy blood alone doth smudge the axe's length.

Immediately outside the Tower of London stands Tower Hill. From that eminence many men – women too – looked their last on the Tower, on London, on life itself. For it was on Tower Hill that scores of victims met death, death that came by the flashing axe, the burning logs, the taut rope. Down through the centuries the names reproach history for the manner in which death was meted out: John Goose, a Lollard, burnt in 1475; four church robbers hanged in 1480, as was Lady Pargitor's manservant for coin clipping in 1538; John Smith, Groom of King Edward's Stirrup, beheaded for treason in 1483, together with William Collingbourne, Sheriff of Wiltshire, hanged, drawn and quartered for composing a verse derogatory to Richard III. Death distinguished not between the highest and the lowest; from Don Pantaleon Sa, brother to the Portuguese Ambassador, beheaded for murder 1654, down to Mary Roberts, Charlotte Gardner and a one-armed soldier, William MacDonald, hanged for rioting in 1780. Many eminent names grace the lists, lords, dukes, archbishops, most of them having been led from their prison cells in the Tower of London by the yeoman warders who handed them

14

over (against a receipt!) to the Sheriff of London and his men at the Tower Gates. Following beheading, the head was spiked on London Bridge as an awful example to all, the body being returned to the Tower for burial within or near the Chapel Royal of St Peter ad Vincula.

It is hardly surprising then that such suffering should manifest itself to those whose duties require them to be near the main gates. There the victims first faced the waiting crowds, the surging multitude of avid spectators; there the grim procession started, to end on the scaffold on the Hill.

And so it was that one night in World War II a sentry patrolling the Tower entrance was suddenly shocked into bloodchilling awareness of figures trooping down the Hill towards him. Clad in quaint uniforms, they slowly advanced. In their midst they bore a rough stretcher. And on the stretcher sprawled a headless body – whilst between arm and torso lay the severed head! Nearer and nearer the grim cortege approached – to fade into nothingness when barely yards away.

The sentry's detailed report was investigated by the authorities with great thoroughness. It was discovered that the uniforms worn by the ghostly figures tallied with those issued to the Sheriff's Men in the Middle Ages, men whose job it was to bring the corpse back for burial; the head being conveyed to London Bridge by river from Tower Steps, the quickest and most customary route. All the reported facts agreed with historical detail – so who are we to doubt it?

The Middle Tower

The Middle Tower

Here the mind's ear is sore press't
To catch but one sweet blessèd breath
Drawn from out an happy heart.
This tower they call the Middle. . . .
What hath become of both the end and start,
And which fine joker hath brought forth
This gloomy riddle?

This, the first tower encountered on entering the castle, dates from 1280, though it was restored in 1717. It was too near the outer walls to be much used as a prison, but the name of one eminent prisoner appears in the ancient records, that of Laurence Shirley, Earl Ferrers. In 1760 he murdered his bailiff Johnson, shooting him with a pistol, for which foul deed he was taken to Tyburn to be hanged. Always elegant, the earl wore silver-embroidered clothes and made his final journey in his own carriage drawn by six horses. His entitlement, as an earl, to be hanged by a silken cord, was denied. He swung from a common hempen rope.

So was it his eccentric spirit which, a few years ago (1977), terrified two painters working within the Middle Tower? In broad daylight they heard the echoing sound of footsteps pacing the battlemented roof above. At first each thought the other was responsible and so was not alarmed. And then, when both were later working together in the same room ... the measured pacing suddenly commenced. With dawning horror their eyes followed the path of the sounds beyond the ceiling – to pause – then to retrace its route.

Assistance was called for, and a thorough search

revealed no *physical* presence nor any hiding-place. No battlements connect this tower with any other. Yet again and again during the next few days the footsteps were heard.

Was it the murderous earl – or some other, unrecorded felon, whose restless soul finds no peace?

Water Lane – Bloody Tower and Wakefield Tower on the left

The Outer Ward

What sweet subtletie thou art,
That takes my heart
And renders it ensnared and palpitating!
Thou art surely of the Gods' creating,
And naught of this unhappy Tower,
The combining of a shining Parenthood art thou,
A very Child of Eos with thy milken brow,
A cradle's wealth grown unto woman now,
The breath of life for which my soul lay waiting.
O dally by the Well Tower yet,
And cull a knot of Bergamot
Within thy garden,
Till my frail grasp betrays me to this Oubliette,
And I am thus by thee and all the World forgot,
Who none would pardon.

Sally port, Byward archway

The area between the inner and outer walls of the Tower of London is known as the Outer Ward. The southernmost stretch, from the Byward Tower to the Salt Tower, is Water Lane, the river Thames once flowing there before the construction of the outer wall in the thirteenth century. The other three sides of the Outer Ward are called the Casemates. These 'vaulted rooms within a fortified place' are stores, workshops and the residences of yeoman warders, their families and other staff. Over the centuries prisoners traversed the Outer Ward on their way to a prison tower or while being escorted to their deaths. It is hardly surprising then that this area has its fair share of occurrences that defy rational explanation.

One night in 1968 a Scots Guards sentry, whose patrol took him from the Byward Tower and Sally Port (a gloomy portal, once the Royal Entrance over the moat) and along to Traitors' Gate, was found in a distressed condition. 'They're following me up and down on my beat,' he gasped fearfully. 'They came out of the Sally Port!' Nothing untoward was discovered – but the sentry had to be relieved of his duty.

Within a year or so yet another visitation occurred,

King Henry VI

farther along Water Lane. In the middle of the night the sentry on duty there rushed into the guardroom. Distraught, the hair on his neck literally bristling, he could only gasp: 'Man in cloak – man in cloak!' He was given medical aid to combat his obviously shocked condition and, when more coherent, he described what he'd seen. A cloaked figure had suddenly emerged from the shadows. The sentry had been about to challenge, but the words had frozen on his lips as he saw that the figure was headless!

On Water Lane stands the Wakefield Tower, one of the most ancient towers within the fortress. Built in the thirteenth century, it has served many uses: entrance to the long demolished Royal Apartments; storehouse of the state treaties and papers; depository of the Crown Jewels and State Regalia. The most gruesome function however was that of a prison, its dungeon being capable of confining scores of doomed wretches within its cold barbaric walls.

The Wakefield's most distinguished prisoner was without doubt King Henry VI. This gentle, learned monarch, fated by birth to wear the Crown, was ill-equipped to be the firm, decisive leader demanded by a country torn by civil strife. As the fortunes swung in the War of the Roses, so Henry VI first ruled from Westminster, then suffered captivity in the Tower. There finally, 'on a Tuesday night 21 May 1471 betwixt xi and xii of the clock, the Duke of Gloster being then at the Tower and many others', the sad king met his end. Whilst praying in the little oratory in the upper chamber of the Wakefield Tower he was 'stikked with a dagger, full of deadly holes' – a dagger, many people

25

believe, wielded by Richard of Gloucester, though no proof exists of this.

And it is said that the king's pale figure has been seen wandering fitfully outside the chamber in which he was so brutally slain – and that the figure appears between eleven o'clock and midnight!

Between the Wakefield Tower and the next, the Lanthorn Tower, runs a high battlemented wall, part of the inner curtain wall. There, centuries ago, stood the Great Hall, abode of Royalty, providing more comfort than did the White Tower. There kings and queens presided over sumptuous banquets, while maids-in-waiting flirted and jesters pranced and joked.

So who – or what – threw stones at a patrolling sentry on a dark still night in October 1978? From the battlements they rattled about his feet. Thrown singly, they hit his boots, one striking his leg – yet there was no wind to dislodge flaking fragments from the coping stone – nor did they fall vertically, but landed five yards or more from the wall's base. When another sentry took over, he too was subjected to similar bombardment. A search revealed nothing – except the realization that there was no access to the top of the sheer wall other than a small door high in the Wakefield Tower, a door not only locked but having a further iron-barred gate secured across it.

No trace of the unseen assailant could be found – but shaken R.A.F. Regiment sentries, and a handful of small stones, bear witness to the playfulness of what long-dead joker?

Facing the Wakefield Tower is Traitors' Gate, the entrance through which the prisoners were brought by boat from their trial at Westminster. Proud princesses, doomed queens, condemned ministers, lords and prelates passed beneath the grim archway, its portcullis raised in readiness, prisoners en route to harsh imprisonment or worse.

Above the archway is St Thomas' Tower, named not as is often thought after St Thomas More but St Thomas a'Becket, Archbishop of Canterbury, for he it is whose ghost is reputed to have appeared when arch and tower were being built.

In 1240 King Henry III, having filched adjoining land in order to increase the defences of his castle, gave orders for a watergate to be built, with a low tower above it. Tradition has it that on Saint George's Day 1240, when the edifice was all but complete, a storm arose and arch and tower collapsed. Work was restarted and proceeded well – until Saint George's Day 1241, when again the building gave way.

The explanation was given by a priest who claimed that he had witnessed the ghost of St Thomas a'Becket striking the stonework with his cross, whilst exclaiming that the defences were not for the benefit of the kingdom but 'for the injury and prejudice of the Londoners, my brethren'. Upon which dire condemnation the arch and tower were reduced to rubble.

Henry III, mindful that it was his grandfather who had caused the death of that 'turbulent priest' Becket, prudently insured himself against ghostly recriminations by including in the new building a small oratory, and naming the building after the indignant martyr, St Thomas.

Earlier this century the then Keeper of the Jewel

Wakefield/Lanthorn battlements, Outer Ward

House, Maj.-Gen. Sir George Younghusband, KCMG, KCIE, CB, resided in St Thomas' Tower. He related having been in a room there, the door of which slowly opened – remained so for a few seconds – then just as gently, closed again. This happened more than once, but nothing more was seen. There have been reports of a monk, wearing a brown habit, moving through the shadows, whilst a more recent occupant and his family recounted instances of having heard in 1974 a soft 'slap slap', as if of monks' sandals moving across a wooden floor – disconcerting to say the least, since the residence had wall to wall carpeting!

Mint Street, that section of the Outer Ward running north from the Byward Tower, is not exempt from eerie happenings. I myself as a yeoman warder going on duty before dawn one morning heard a sentry approaching along Mint Street. 'Has anyone passed you?' the sentry, a Scots Guardsman, asked. I paused, then queried the sentry's departure from the usual beat. 'I heard an unearthly shriek,' he explained. 'It came from along there.' He pointed in the direction from which I had come 'And after the yell I heard the sound of running footsteps!'

He spoke calmly and was obviously not a man given to flights of fancy – yet I had walked alone along the dark, silent street for over two hundred yards, having heard and seen nothing.

Not all the instances have occurred in the open air. Footsteps have been heard ascending the stairs within one of the houses set in the thickness of the outer wall, footsteps sounding when no one but the listening resident was in the house. Later, in an upper room, my

'Traitors' Gate and St Thomas's Tower

wife felt the overwhelming presence of 'someone else', a sensation accompanied by a feeling of chilling evil. At last, determined not to panic, she could nevertheless withstand it no longer, and had to retreat hurriedly to find the comfort of neighbours and the everyday bustle of the world.

Other residents have heard the crying of a baby coming from an upper room. Thinking it was their child they investigated. Theirs lay sleeping peacefully in its cot. But the eerie crying continued – from where? from what?

Within the same house a yeoman warder, whilst standing in the hall one evening, suddenly became aware of a man a few feet away, by the front door. No mediaeval figure this; no ruff, no doublet, no foppish Court dress even – yet old fashioned in a way, for he wore a grey suit cut in the utility style of the 1940s. As the yeoman warder turned in surprise, the figure vanished. This happened in 1977.

No records exist of any tragedy in that house – except that only yards away stood until recently the ill-fated rifle range where enemy spies were executed by firing squad during the two World Wars. Behind the high walls of the Tower of London they faced death bravely. Who knows when their spirits found peace?

Mint Street, Outer Ward

The Bloody Tower

Stay ye near the tower, the Bloody Tower, at ten,
And ye shall hear a cry,
A great Amen,
That lifts the very Raven's savage head,
And wakes the sleeping servant in his bed.
'God preserve King Henry!' is the shout,
And by warder 'gainst strong guard the keys are carried,
As if iron into palm the twain are married. . . .
    And the while the candlelamp it goes not out.
So praise ye all that God preserves King Hal,
Foolhardy is the one whose voice is weak,
But if ye have aught else on which to speak. . . .
    Wait till the candlelamp it goeth out!

Bloody Tower Arch

The Inner Ward is the area surrounding the White Tower, and is bordered by the inner wall. For many centuries, when Royalty resided in the White Tower and the Royal Apartments, the inner ward was for the exclusive use of Royalty and the nobles of the court. Also within the protection of the inner wall were stored the nation's armoury, the State Papers, and the Regalia and Jewels. During these centuries there was only one entrance to the inner ward, a heavily guarded archway beneath a gatehouse known originally as the Garden Tower (it overlooked the gardens of the Lieutenant's Lodgings) but later as the Bloody Tower. Situated only yards from Traitors' Gate, it served admirably as a prison for princes and knights, bishops and judges.

Here, in Queen Mary's reign, languished Thomas Cranmer, Archbishop of Canterbury, Bishop Latimer of Winchester and Nicholas Ridley, Bishop of London. Opposing the Pope's supremacy, they were condemned as heretics and later burnt to death at Oxford.

Here, in the same reign, John Dudley, Duke of Northumberland, was confined for attempting to make his daughter-in-law, Lady Jane Grey, Queen of

The Bloody Tower

England. He perished beneath the axe on Tower Hill, the vast crowd cheering as he died.

Judge Jeffries, the Hanging Judge of the Monmouth Rebellion in 1685, eventually caught by the mob, was placed in the Bloody Tower for his own protection – where he drank himself to death with copious draughts of brandy.

The Bloody Tower also heard the whispering of evil conspirators, when Sir Thomas Overbury survived fearful poisoning for over four months. He had sought to persuade his friend Robert Carr not to marry the vicious Countess of Essex, but he under-estimated her influence and malice. Finally her poisonous concoctions took effect, and in the Bloody Tower he died a horrifying death.

But if the stones could speak, surely they would lament the deaths of the two little princes in 1483. Confined, it is said, in the upper chamber of the Bloody Tower, the two small boys, twelve-year-old King Edward V and his nine-year-old brother Richard Duke of York, were taken from their mother's care into the custody of their uncle, Richard Duke of Gloucester. Placed in the Bloody Tower, they were never seen again. The country could not continue without a ruler, and so the Duke of Gloucester became King Richard III.

Tradition states that one boy was smothered, the other stabbed to death. Skeletons discovered in 1674 beneath an external stairway of the White Tower were assumed to be theirs.

And so their two small ghosts, hand in hand, clad in white nightgowns, have been seen around the Bloody

Sir Walter Raleigh

Tower, a sight for pity and compassion rather than terror.

Be they innocent children or worldly adults, the Bloody Tower spared none, and surely no one proved more brave than Sir Walter Raleigh. An adventurer, a scientist, the favourite of Queen Elizabeth, he could do little wrong. But the next monarch, James I, had no time for men of Raleigh's sophisticated calibre. Accused of treasonable plotting, Raleigh was soon the occupant of the Bloody Tower, a confinement which lasted thirteen years. He would stroll on Raleigh's Walk, the battlemented wall adjoining his prison; dressed always in the height of fashion, he was popular with the people, with rich merchants, ambassadors and learned men. But as the years dragged by, the cold of the stones and the dampness of the river mists sapped his vitality, and rheumatism racked his ageing joints. King James, anxious to conclude a peace pact with Philip of Spain, acceded to Philip's vengeful demand for Raleigh's death, Raleigh who had plundered so much gold from Spanish galleons and colonies.

Eventually, on 24th October 1618, after years of deprivation, Raleigh was awakened by a yeoman warder and told his fate. Peter, his valet, attempted to help him to prepare, to comb his hair. Raleigh, undaunted to the end, retorted: 'Let them comb it that shall have it!' Taken to Old Palace Yard at Westminster, he met death bravely as the axe descended.

His phantom, then, surely has greater claim than any other to return to the scene of his long imprisonment. Over the years it has been reportedly seen flitting noiselessly through the forbidding rooms of the Bloody Tower; seen too on moonlit nights by those whose duties take them past Raleigh's Walk, his ghostly figure floating along the battlements.

In Raleigh's time the Walk extended to the Lieutenant's Lodgings. Now part of those battlements are incorporated in houses built a century or so later, houses occupied by yeoman warders and their families. And since 1976 one wife in particular will always have cause to remember that her bathroom is positioned where Raleigh promenaded. Deciding to have a bath, she leant over to turn on the taps. Next minute a hand brushed gently over the small of her back! Instinctively she straightened up, turning to chide her husband – then caught her breath as she remembered that he was Watchman for the night and had left the house hours ago! However, yeoman warders' wives are not given to swoons or the vapours; 'Oh, stop it, Raleigh!' she exclaimed and, undaunted, continued with her ablutions!

Incidents such as this are not restricted to night-time, nor do they occur only to officials or residents of the fortress. In August 1970 a young visitor to the Bloody Tower saw a long-haired woman wearing an ankle-length black velvet dress, standing by an open window. She wore a white cap, and around her neck hung a large, gold medallion. As the visitor stared, the figure faded away.

Intrigued, the visitor returned some weeks later – only to see the apparition again, in the same place! No longer shocked by the unexpected, she was able to describe in detail the apparel of the ghost.

'Princes in the Bloody Tower' (an artist's impression from an Edwardian postcard)

The mediaeval records are understandably incomplete, but for all we know, one of the many women who suffered imprisonment may well have been locked up behind the Bloody Tower's ancient, creaking doors.

Two R.A.F. Regiment sentries on guard in October 1978 will not easily forget their tour of duty. On a still, moonless night, just after midnight, with never an autumn leaf stirring, they patrolled beneath the Bloody Tower arch. For no apparent reason they paused, feeling eerie apprehension, the hairs at the back of their necks bristling – and then their short capes billowed upward, almost covering their faces, as an icy breeze suddenly blew through the archway – a rush of cold air which died away as rapidly and as inexplicably as it had arrived.

Later that night their sergeant traversed the grim forbidding archway en route to the Waterloo Block. To his right the floodlights illuminated the ancient thirteenth-century wall built to stand high and impenetrable, guarding the approaches to the White Tower. Now it was crumbling, pierced by gaping holes once arrow slits and loops.

The sergeant paused, his attention attracted by a shadow he could see through a hole in the nearest end of the wall adjoining the Wakefield Tower. He stared – then his eyes widened with disbelief as the shadow moved ... vanished ... only to reappear at the next hole! Hardly pausing, the shape slipped past each gaping aperture, gliding silently along behind the crumbling wall. Yet when the sergeant reached the far end, nothing was to be seen on the wide expanse of grass stretching behind the White Tower!

Tower Green

If 'tis seen, men say 'tis not.
If 'tis heard, men say the lot
Of all fools is a simple-mindedness
Beyond belief.
So why hold faith in aught
But candle-flame that burneth,
Roasting-spit that turneth,
Lover's heart that yearneth?
These are plausible, men saith. . . .
So keep unto thyself thy tale
Of yester e'en's ethereal wraith!

Tower Green

A central garden, sheltered by plane trees, is known as Tower Green. It is bounded on the east by the White Tower and the Chapel Royal of St Peter ad Vincula forms its northernmost side. To the west squats the Beauchamp Tower, while its southern border is the Queen's House, originally the Lieutenant's Lodgings – since 1530 the residence of the officer in charge of the Tower of London.

In such a pleasant oasis it is easy to imagine the royal levees, the parties and merrymaking which must have taken place here during the centuries when the Tower of London was a Royal Residence. Yet one small enclosure on Tower Green constantly reminds us that this is where the private scaffold stood, the five-foot high wooden platform, draped in black, strewn with straw. There, witnessed by the Royal Court and dignitaries of the City of London, perished those whose only crime was to incur a king's wounded pride or be thought a dangerous rival.

Before 1536 executions, even of women, were not infrequent; infidelity too, was hardly a rarity. Yet the punishment of death for alleged unfaithfulness – and that in the person of a Queen of England – was

Queen Anne Boleyn

unimaginable. That such an event *did* happen has never ceased to horrify and appal subsequent generations.

Anne Boleyn, second wife of Henry VIII, had been queen two brief years when she was accused of infidelity and treason and sentenced to be 'either burnt or beheaded on the green within the Tower as his Majesty in his pleasure should think fit'. Confined in the Lieutenant's Lodgings for four days, she was led out to the private execution site. Strangely enough she was to be beheaded by the sword – a rare weapon of execution in English history, but infinitely preferable to the axe. The latter was a cumbersome and ill-balanced weapon, its primitive design often necessitating more than one stroke.

Anne mounted the steps and knelt upright, there being no block when the sword was employed. The French headsman, black clad, stepped forward. Her attention being distracted by his assistant, Anne mercifully failed to see the flashing blade as, with one stroke, her head was severed. In accordance with custom, the executioner held her head high – and the gathered assembly gasped in horror as the eyes and lips continued to move! Her pitiful remains were ensconced in an old arrow chest and buried beneath the altar in the Chapel Royal of St Peter ad Vincula on Tower Green.

It is hardly surprising, therefore, that through the centuries apparitions purporting to be those of the doomed queen have been seen, even by those most prosaic and level-headed human beings, soldiers of the British Army.

In 1864 a sentry of the King's Royal Rifle Corps on

Council Chamber in the Queen's House

duty at the Queen's House saw, through the swirling river mist, a white figure. He challenged and, receiving no reply, attacked – only to drive his bayonet through the spectre! Being found in a state of collapse, he was court-martialled but two witnesses at the window of the Bloody Tower corroborated his story and he was acquitted. The phantom figure was seen by other sentries in later years, gaining the sentry post an evil reputation.

Still in the last century, a yeoman warder swore under oath to seeing a bluish form hovering, a shape which then seemed to move towards the Queen's House, whilst in 1933 a guardsman reported seeing a headless woman floating towards him near the Bloody Tower.

Within the Queen's House, long a prison for royal and important personalities as well as being the Lieutenant's residence, many an eerie experience has been reported. Across the ancient timbered floors walks the 'Grey Lady'. Only a woman will ever discover her secret – for she has never been seen by a man. In the 1970s the figure of a man in mediaeval dress was seen drifting along an upper corridor, whilst in the same decade firm footsteps were frequently heard ascending a rear stairway. So convincing were these sounds that eventually two residents investigated. On hearing the measured tread, one resident went instantly to the foot of the stairs, his companion going to the top. Slowly they moved along the stairs – to meet no one but the other!

Late in 1978 an American guest in the house heard religious chanting. It was midnight, and the faint

The Gunpowder Plot conspirators

music and voices continued for some minutes. Assuming it to be from a radio or similar equipment, she mentioned it casually the next day – only to be told that no music had been played as late as that. The same slow religious chant had been heard on a previous occasion by a resident passing by the house.

A room adjoining that in which Anne Boleyn passed her last few days has a particularly unearthly atmosphere, being noticeably colder than other rooms in the house. A peculiar perfumed smell lingers in the air, and such is the brooding menace of the room that no unaccompanied girl or young child is ever permitted to sleep in it, for in the past those who were have woken to feel that they were being slowly suffocated!

Across Tower Green is the Chapel Royal of St Peter ad Vincula, and an instance some years ago of lights burning therein led the Officer of the Guard to investigate. Peering in through the window, he stared unbelieving at the spectacle confronting him. Along the aisle, between the tombs, moved a procession of spectral figures, knights and their ladies. They were led by a female who, he averred, resembled Anne Boleyn, and they moved towards the altar beneath which her pitiful remains had been buried centuries before. Even as he stared the vision faded and the chapel darkened, leaving the officer alone in the deepening shadows of Tower Green.

Of the women who perished so violently on the private scaffold, surely none suffered more terribly – nor more undeservedly – than Margaret Pole, Countess of Salisbury. Over seventy years of age, innocent of all crime, the countess was slain as an act of

Chapel Royal, St Peter ad Vincula

vengeance by King Henry VIII. The countess' son, Cardinal Pole, from the safe haven of France, reviled Henry's religious beliefs. Retribution – and the axe – descended on his mother. On the scaffold the countess proclaimed her innocence. She refused to kneel over the block and she challenged the axeman to 'remove her head as best he could'. Pursuing her around the block, the axeman is said to have literally hacked her to death in a welter of blood.

Over the centuries it seems as if her proud Plantagenet spirit still shrieks defiance to the sombre skies. On the anniversaries of her brutal execution, her ghost is reported to run round the scaffold site pursued by the spectral axeman, the bloodstained axe brandished aloft.

One night in 1975 personnel in the Waterloo Block overlooking the Green were roused in the early hours by the sound of piercing screams. This was confirmed by men on duty in the Byward Tower, and a few nights later the guardsman patrolling the rear of the Waterloo Block also reported that just before dawn he too heard high-pitched screaming from the direction of the Green. Nothing was found.

Could it really have been the death cries of the hideously mutilated countess?

RE CORDS

Singular Execution of the Countess of Salisbury in 15.p.

cruikshank del

The Beauchamp Tower

Heaven send us open weather,
For if I stay thus so shut up,
With no walk upon the battlements,
Then shall I lose my looks, my wits,
And aught else of value
That the good Lord gave me.
'Tis not much when I take air and exercise.
The guards and women there all crowd the way.
But I can stretch both foot and eye,
And see to where the river's sheen
Doth mock the sky.
   So I do say. . . .
   Heaven send us open weather,
   That God and I and London Town
   May stand together.

The Beauchamp
Tower

On the west side of Tower Green, overlooking the scaffold site, stands the Beauchamp Tower. Because of its proximity to the Lieutenant's Lodgings it became one of the more 'popular' prison towers, favouring those of noble birth and high estate. Not that much comfort was provided: a fire, some candles, rushes spread on the floor, these did little to compensate for the open arrow slits and cold, thick walls.

Originally the prison room and the living quarters of its guardian, the yeoman warder, on the top floor, could only be reached via the battlements from the Bell Tower, the latter being integral with the Lieutenant's Lodgings (now the Queen's House). The present doorway was a later addition; in earlier times such an aperture would have weakened the defences, and in any case it would not have been seemly for prisoners to have been conducted through the Inner Ward, the precincts of the nobles and the Royal Family. The lower chambers, then, were dungeons, cramped and gloomy cells secured by heavy doors, approached by spiral stairs from above.

Over the centuries the State Prison Room, on the first floor, housed many prisoners. In them the flame

Elizabeth's Walk

of hope burned bright, the hope that a change of monarch, a change of policy, could bring about their release. For a great number of them, however, it was not to be; after years of captivity they were led out, to face the baying mob, the black-clad axeman. Some did survive, to have titles and estates bestowed on them anew. A grim gamble, with Fate tossing the dice!

During their imprisonment time hung heavy. Many of these were men of breeding and of letters, skilled in Latin, versed in the Scriptures. And there, locked away in the great fortress, having ceased to exist so far as the outside world was concerned, they carved inscriptions on the walls. Proud family crests, pitiful pleas of innocence, religious quotations, even wry witticisms adorn the stonework, mute messages from those who lived from day to day under the shadow of violent execution.

The instrument they used for inscribing was in all probability the dagger. Forks were not invented until the seventeenth century; before that men carried daggers with which to cut their food and convey it to their mouths. It was of little use in an escape bid. The century of the hostage is the twentieth century; when almost any sacrifice is made to save a human life. But in the Middle Ages life was cheap and a prisoner who, holding his warder hostage and demanding freedom, would have been told to go ahead – the Lieutenant had many more warders with which to replace the one stabbed! And should the prisoner employ his dagger to commit suicide, it would simply save the axeman a job.

Among those who left their marks in the stone is

59

Philip Howard, Earl of Arundel. A devout Catholic, he was imprisoned in 1585 accused of aiding the Jesuits and, later, of praying for the success of the Spanish Armada in its attempted invasion of these islands. Queen Elizabeth spared his life, even offering him his freedom if he would forsake his religion. He refused. For ten years he was held prisoner, then died, in his fortieth year, in the Beauchamp Tower.

One of the more famous occupants of the State Prison Room was Lord Guildford Dudley, son of the Duke of Northumberland. The duke, adviser to the ailing King Edward VI, arranged for Guildford to marry the king's cousin Lady Jane Grey, and then recommended to the King that she was the person most suited to succeed to the throne. She was eligible by birth, and the Duke was a very ambitious man. To have his son and daughter-in-law King and Queen of England would have given him immeasurable power and wealth.

The young king agreed to this, then conveniently died. Whereupon Northumberland brought Guildford and his wife to the White Tower and proclaimed Lady Jane Grey Queen of England. But he was completely unaware that the majority of the country wanted, not Jane, but the dead king's sister, Mary Tudor. So overwhelming the support for Mary, so troublesome the uprisings by those few who supported Jane, that the days of the uncrowned queen were numbered. She was beheaded on Tower Green; her father-in-law Northumberland begged for mercy and promised to renounce his faith, to embrace Catholicism. Mary Tudor permitted him to do so, the ceremony being enacted in St John's Chapel in the White Tower. Then she had him executed!

Young Guildford and his four brothers were all imprisoned in the Beauchamp Tower, where two carvings of the name 'Jane' have been found inscribed on the walls. Of the five brothers, one died therein, three were released, and Guildford perished beneath the axe on Tower Hill. His headless body, 'dragged in a carre' across the cobbles, was entombed in the Chapel Royal of St Peter ad Vincula on Tower Green.

As with other towers, so the Beauchamp has its share of supernatural happenings. The battlements connecting the Bell Tower with the Beauchamp had the name 'Prisoners' Walk' and later 'Elizabeth's Walk'. Here those prisoners who were not close confined (that is, fettered and chained within their cells), were allowed to exercise, and even catch a glimpse of the outside world.

Hardly surprising then, that a Tower guide should see a man wearing cavalier-type clothing moving along those battlements. This sighting occurred during the afternoon and, as Elizabeth's Walk cannot be seen from the Inner Ward because of the houses obscuring it, the figure could only have been seen from outside the Tower of London, from the area of the front gates.

The apparition could well have been that of James, Duke of Monmouth who in 1685 led the ill-fated Monmouth's Rebellion against the King's forces. Defeated, he was imprisoned in the Bell Tower and doubtless exercised on Elizabeth's Walk. After his trial he was taken to Tower Hill and there, before a

James, Duke of Monmouth

multitude of spectators, gave the axeman a few gold guineas to make a quick job of the execution.

'Pray do your business well,' he said. 'Do not serve me as you did my Lord Russell; I have heard that you struck him three or four times – if you strike me twice I cannot promise not to move.'

The inducement availed him little; the axeman took five blows to sever his head, much to the fury of the crowd. It is related that the head was subsequently sewn back on to the torso so that a portrait could be painted, the join being hidden by a scarf.

Inside the Beauchamp itself, eerie gasps have been heard from time to time, and ornaments unaccountably change their position within the room. An old story recounts how the spectre of Lord Guildford Dudley was seen, shedding ghostly tears, drifting around the State Prison Room. Poor Dudley, so soon to be parted from his young queen-wife, to be reunited after death beneath the cold altar stones of St Peter's Chapel.

The White Tower

Planted as he was in manhood's strength,
Upon the Broadwalk where his eyes had length
Enough to compass majestie and might,
He made a study of the nation's vile disorder.
'Ever like this it has been,' he pondered,
'Ever the arrow's line has wandered,
'Till the bow is slack and still,
'And the shaft without a flight.
'But look you, London,
'Look you God's environ'd world,
'To where the Union Flag at sun-up is unfurl'd,
'There by the White Tower's glowering impound,'
'Is stood a Yeoman Warder strongly to his ground,
'And 'neath his breast in happy pride encurl'd,
'The throbbing heart of England still is found.'

Standing proudly in the Inner Ward, dominating Tower Green, the Broadwalk and indeed all the other towers, is the Norman Keep – the White Tower. Ninety-two feet high, its battlemented roof is capped by four turrets, a roof strong enough to support the weight of the many cannon which defended the Keep in the reign of Henry VIII.

Like most Norman keeps it originally had but a single entrance, situated one floor above ground level. Should all outer defences fall, the men-at-arms would then hack away the external wooden steps and, out of reach of battering rams could continue to hold out against attack. The White Tower was self-sufficient even in that vital commodity, water, a well in the basement providing ample supplies.

Not content with the protection of the moat, draw-bridges and portcullis, two surrounding walls and a small resident army of troops, the Royal Family lived as far away as possible from any attack – on the uppermost floor of the White Tower. Adjoining their apartments was the Great Council Chamber, where the issues of the day were resolved, usually by the king. The White Tower was primarily a castle built for defence rather than a palace for luxury, and so the narrow passages could be defended by just two men, and the spiral stair was designed 'clockwise ascending' so that a right-handed defender had superiority wielding a sword against a right-hander attacking up the stairs. Comfort there was little, windows being small for protection but, unglazed, admitted the bitter winds blowing along the river. Tapestries on the walls, straw strewn floors, log fires crackling in the fireplaces; primitive conditions indeed, but at least the occupants were safe from attack. In those days that was all important.

The Banqueting Chamber and the quarters of the nobles of the Court occupied the next floor down, while the reception floor housed the men-at-arms and personal staff.

Nor was the spiritual side of life neglected; the White Tower possesses one of the most perfect examples of a Norman chapel, the Chapel Royal of St John the Evangelist. Here royalty worshipped; here the Order of the Bath took place in which potential knights prepared themselves before their accolade; here too, Lady Jane Grey was proclaimed Queen of England, the girl so young to be queen, so soon to die; and Mary Tudor plighted her troth to King Philip of Spain.

The lowest floor, half underground, housed the armoury and kitchens, the dungeons and the torture chamber. No doors or windows there, in those days – behind the fifteen-feet thick walls, accessible only via the spiral stairs from above, the prisoners were incarcerated. There, in the darkness and squalor, men – and women – suffered the agonies of the rack, the fearsome constrictions of Skeffington's Daughter, its iron bands contorting the body beyond endurance. For while coronation processions rich in panoply and trappings did indeed start from the White Tower; while festive carousals filled the Banqueting Chamber, life in the fortress was only revelry and feasting for those in the sovereign's favour. Others, who had forfeited the royal trust, forfeited their freedom – and later, their heads.

From the very roof to the dungeons, the White Tower has witnessed violence and death. Kings and princes, lords and ladies, even common soldiers looked their last on the world there. During the Civil War a Royalist soldier was hotly chased up the spiral stairs by a Roundhead. Having lost his sword, desperately the Royalist dropped to his knee and, tripping his pursuer, seized him and hurled him through the window, the Roundhead crashing to his death on the Broadwalk below.

Centuries earlier, in 1215, the country had groaned beneath the harsh rule of King John. But, tradition has it, he had more to concern him than the suffering of the masses. Despite being married, he was determined to possess Maud FitzWalter, 'Fair Maud', daughter of Baron FitzWalter of Baynards Castle. She repulsed his every advance and so, not to be denied, he had her abducted and locked up in the round turret of the White Tower. Her father protested so vehemently that the king exiled him and his family to France and then, all obstacles removed, continued his assault of Fair Maud's virtue! Though caged and helpless, Maud defied him – whereupon he caused a poisoned egg to be sent to her in her food. She ate it – and died there in the bitter cold loneliness of the high turret.

Much later her father managed to return home, to find the country on the verge of revolution. Mustering the other barons to the cause, he led them against the King, ultimately forcing him to endorse the Magna Carta. And so it could be said that the document which gave the English their freedom originated from a poisoned egg in the round turret of the White Tower. Perhaps Maud's life was not sacrificed entirely in vain.

High on the battlements in 1234 Gruffydd Prince of Wales sought to escape by lowering himself from the roof by means of a rope. But the rope broke and Grufydd plunged to instant death, being found the next morning 'his head and neck crushed between his shoulder blades'. His son, Llewelyn, also a prisoner, later escaped and continued to fight the English. Captured in 1282, he was executed and his head was mounted on a spike and exhibited in London while bells rang and crowds cheered. It was adorned with an ivy wreath, thus fulfilling the ancient prophecy that a Welsh prince would one day be crowned in London! The head was then attached to a turret of the White Tower, near the spot from whence his father had previously fallen to such a hideous death. Truly a warning to all, that escape didn't always mean freedom.

Even the top floor, domicile of the Royal Family, was not spared its share of horror. In the adjoining Council Chamber one day in June 1485 Richard, Duke of Gloucester (later King Richard III) presided at a Council Meeting. Requiring to dispose of Lord

Hastings, he accused him of treason and witchcraft. 'By St Paul!' he exclaimed, 'I will not dine till I have seen thy head off!'

The wretched Hastings was hustled down the spiral stair and out on the Tower Green. A log of timber served as the block; without trial or comfort of clergy his head was struck off – then shown to Richard ere he sat down to his midday meal.

Most violence, however, occurred in the dungeons. Here, underground, in the reign of Edward I, six hundred Jews, men and their families, were crowded together in appalling conditions. Public opinion strongly against them, they were accused of coin clipping, scraping metal from the rims of coins, a profitable crime. They were imprisoned for some months, and no fewer than two hundred and sixty-seven were eventually hanged.

Chivalry may have played a part on the mediaeval battlefield; it certainly had no place in the torture chamber of the White Tower. If a prisoner could be forced to divulge secrets which might incriminate a rival, it mattered not whether that prisoner was man or woman. In 1545 Anne Askew was accused of heresy by those who hoped that her confession would implicate Henry VIII's Queen Katherine Parr. Anne, a highly intelligent woman, was a zealous Protestant, a dangerous belief to hold in those bigoted days. She had been a friend of the queen, who held the same religious opinions – and so powerful enemies struck.

Arrested, imprisoned, questioned at length by Bonner, Bishop of London, she parried his accusations with shrewd responses. But it availed her little; she was sent to the White Tower and there, in the flickering lantern-light of the torture chamber she was racked unmercifully for over an hour. She confessed nothing. At last, her limbs stretched beyond endurance, almost senseless with agony, she was carried back to her cell. A short time later she was taken on a cart to Smithfield. There, before a vast crowd of callous, jeering onlookers, she was burned to death at the stake. But someone, somehow, felt pity for the poor tortured woman, for a bag of gunpowder inserted among the fiercely burning logs brought her merciful release from the searing flames.

Gunpowder provided relief for Anne Askew; it spelt only doom to Guy Fawkes and his companions in 1605. Caught attempting to blow up the Houses of Parliament, Fawkes was yet another whose tongue – and joints – were loosened as the rack pulleys creaked and the ropes stretched remorselessly. After half an hour's excruciating torment he was a broken man, naming names, admitting everything. The other plotters were rounded up and the ringleaders were put to that most terrible of deaths, being hanged, drawn and quartered.

If the supernatural atmosphere of the White Tower was a stage, then we would certainly not want for a cast of players. Those already mentioned are but a few who would claim star parts, and even if their apparitions failed to materialize, surely the intensity of their sufferings could well echo down the centuries, just as their screams must have reverberated along the passages and stairways of their grim prison.

Instances have been reported by sentries patrolling

at night, instances of hearing screams and stifled cries of pain through the heavy doors at the base of the White Tower. And not so many years ago, soldiers reported seeing the huge shadow of an axe spreading across Tower Green, to stand menacingly erect, silhouetted against the walls of the White Tower.

A body of men with even stronger nerves than the sentries – if such were possible – are the Department of the Environment Custody Guards, one of whose many tasks is to check security within the White Tower during the night hours. In the brooding silence of the vast shadowy rooms it is not easy to dismiss a creaking noise as just an old floorboard, that cold breath of air as just a draught – especially when all windows are tightly secured! And as for a faint smell of incense, once experienced – in 1975 – by a security warden – rubbish! Though remembering that high prelates did attend the interrogation of heretics under torture, why should there not be the ghost of the aroma of incense?

Of *course* there couldn't be eyes watching malevolently through the slits in that knight's helmet – but what would *you* see if you turned round really quickly?

Oh, no, the White Tower at night is no place for the faint of heart – in any century.

The Martin Tower

Here in the midmost of a modern day,
When clarity of thought and deed hold sway,
What parcel of fancies with the thread undone
Can set man's dignity off at the run,
Wailing and sobbing as a babe at the knee,
To shudder at sights none other can see.

The Martin Tower

At the north-east corner of the inner wall stands the Martin Tower, a tower of many ghostly legends. At the turn of the century it was reported that a figure in white walked the upper room, to the great alarm of the yeoman warders – and even in these times there are some workmen who are reluctant to work inside it, such is its eerie atmosphere. George Boleyn, Anne Boleyn's brother, was imprisoned in the Martin Tower, later being hanged, drawn and quartered on the vengeful instructions of King Henry VIII.

Yet one man whose spirit is reputed to linger around this tower is one who was acquitted and released! The intrigue of the Gunpowder Plot in 1605 involved many names. A few are well known, such as Guy Fawkes, Ambrose Rookwood, Father Gerard; many are less known, Winter, Wright, Kay. One such latter was Thomas Percy, an active conspirator in the Plot, a man related to Henry Percy, ninth Earl of Northumberland. Upon the discovery of the plot, charges were laid against the earl, alleging his complicity. And so this elderly and learned gentleman was confined in the Martin Tower for no less than sixteen years. That his confinement was not particularly arduous is evidenced

75

by the fact that his family lived with him for some of that time, and that he formed a scientific and literary circle within the Tower of London, other erudite prisoners, among them Sir Walter Raleigh, visiting the Martin Tower to debate the finer points of the times with the 'Wizard Earl' as he was known.

The Earl was subsequently released in 1620 after paying a £30,000 fine, truly a fortune in those days. Whilst confined he took his exercise on 'Northumberland's Walk', the battlements each side of the Martin Tower. Although he suffered neither torture nor sudden death, his ghost was seen, late in the last century, by sentries who, terrified, would only mount guard in pairs. Not only that, but the innocent passer-by has on occasion felt unseen hands push him – or her! – down the steps by the Martin Tower.

Not all happenings end so mildly. Indeed one poor unfortunate snapped beneath the strain of such an experience – and paid with his life. He was a sentry who, in January 1815, was on patrol before the arched doorway of the Martin Tower (then the Jewel House). Midnight was striking when, to his sudden horror, he saw the figure of a huge bear emerge from beneath the door. Desperately he lunged with his bayonet, only to have the weapon pass through the shape and embed itself in the oaken door. His comrades, hearing the commotion, hurried to the spot – to find him stretched unconscious on the ground.

Questioned the next day by the Jewel House Keeper, Mr Edmund Lenthal Swifte, the sentry was 'trembling and haunted by fear, a man changed beyond recognition'. Within two days he was dead –

during which time his bayonet still pierced the ancient timbers of the door he had died guarding.

And such are the quirks of fate that it was Lenthal Swifte himself who was involved in one of the eeriest emanations ever to occur within the fortress. One cold night in October 1817 the Keeper of The Crown Jewels was having supper in the dining room of the Martin Tower. The three doors to the room were closed and heavy curtains shrouded the two windows. His family, consisting of his wife, their son aged seven, and his wife's sister, sat round the oblong table, his wife facing the fireplace. Two candles illuminated the scene, though doubtless a fire burned bright as well. Mrs Swifte raised a glass of wine and water to her lips, then suddenly exclaimed, 'Good God! What is that?' Swifte looked up – to see what appeared to be a glass cylinder about three inches in diameter floating above the table; within it bluish-white fluids swirled and writhed. It hovered then, moving slowly along, passed behind his wife. Immediately she cowered, covering her shoulder with both hands. 'Oh Christ!' she shrieked. 'It has seized me!' That she felt *something* was evident, for no mirror faced her, only the fireplace, yet her sister and son saw nothing of the appearance. Mr Swifte, filled with horror, sprang to his feet and hurled his chair at the hovering apparition – to see the tube cross the upper end of the table and disappear in the recess of the opposite window.

Later Mr Swifte, an intelligent and highly responsible official, set down a detailed report of the occurrence. Never once when recounting it during later years did he change a single detail – or deny the terror

77

which imprinted itself on his memory that dark night in the Martin Tower.

Not all visitations in that locality are, however, hostile. South of the Martin Tower and connected to it by Northumberland's Walk lies the Constable Tower. Once, long ago, the residence of the Constable of the Tower of London, it is now the home of a yeoman warder and his wife.

Over the years since 1973 a 'presence' has manifested itself. This spirit has nudged the wife's arm so determinedly that the pen spluttered sideways across the paper! The occupants of the Constable Tower are immediately aware of its arrival, because it is heralded by a strong 'horseman' smell, a compounded odour of leather, of sweating horseflesh, – that of a rider who, having just dismounted after a long hard gallop, strides into his home.

'He's here again!' comments the yeoman warder, and his wife nods agreement. They're not apprehensive for, far from being hostile, this spirit generates a warm friendliness – a rarity indeed in the Tower of London!

The Salt Tower

There is a merrie England
Of a compact sphere,
That dwelleth here
Within the Tower of London.
Merrie enough if there be gain
At plain man's torture,
Lover's pain,
Liar's shriek, honesty's prayer,
And the signet of blood on floor and stair.
So pause as ye go, think as ye stand,
Of the fluttering kerchief,
The enfeebled hand.
Did ye not see them?
Say now for sure,
For a ghost made not welcome,
Appeareth the more.

The Salt Tower guards the south-east corner of the Inner Ward. Originally it could only be entered via the battlements, as could the Beauchamp Tower and others. The lower room therefore was a dark and noisome dungeon, half underground, though the upper cells were little better. Dating from the thirteenth century, it too confined many prisoners behind its grim walls. Most of them were Jesuit priests, caught in the religious persecutions of the sixteenth and early seventeenth centuries. One such was Henry Walpole, a young Englishman. He had witnessed the execution of Jesuit priests, men who had been terribly tortured for their Catholic beliefs. This spectacle, at a time when this country was at war with Spain, only inspired Walpole to take over their task. Already converted, he became a Jesuit and in 1589 he joined the Spanish Army in Flanders, as a chaplain. Four years later he returned to further the Catholic cause. He was captured and sent to the Tower of London. There every effort was made to extract information from him. Despite being racked many times he remained silent. He was imprisoned in the Salt Tower and there on the cold stone walls he carved his name and those of the saints who gave him the strength and fortitude of soul to endure the torture and confinement. At last, in 1595, he was taken to York where he was tried and executed, probably by being burned alive.

One late afternoon in 1973 a yeoman warder visited the Salt Tower. He had recently been reading a book about the Jesuits, a book which discredited their principles and condemned them as traitors. He mounted the narrow winding stairs and, alone in the gathering gloom, he studied the inscriptions so laboriously carved by tortured hands. Without warning, a sudden glow illuminated the prison chamber – and he felt some 'thing' touch him on the back of the neck! For one moment he stood frozen with fear – then hardly knowing what he was doing he fled down the spiral stairs and out of the arched doorway. It was some considerable time later that he was able to control his racing pulses and calm down. Yeoman warders are not given to imagining things – but the book, needless to say, is no longer in his possession!

Nor is it only sensations which pervade this particular tower. On 12th January 1957, soon after midnight, two guardsmen on sentry duty saw a shapeless white form high up on the battlemented roof of the Salt Tower. As they stared unbelievingly, the apparition lingered – then slowly faded away!

Just a few yards from the Salt Tower stands the new History Gallery. Before its foundations were laid, excavations took place alongside the base of the Roman Wall there. At a depth of more than fifteen feet a grave was discovered in 1976, a grave containing the skeleton of a young man. He lay on his back, his knees slightly bent, his hands crossed before him. His head was tilted to one side – and in the skull gaped an ugly hole.

Who was he, this Iron Age youth who had lain there for nearly two thousand years, making his the earliest human remains to have been found to date within the City? How different was his life from ours? How violent his death – and why?

And will his spirit return, to drift phantomlike in the dim recesses of the History Gallery, to reproach those who dared to violate his last resting place?

Conclusion

I would smile me a smile,
Sing me a song,
Dance me a dance
As the day is long.
But who would I partner,
Death or delight?
Now that is the question. . . .
That is the fright!

Most of the uncanny happenings within the Tower of London have been experienced by sentries and yeoman warders. This is quite understandable, they being on duty in the Tower grounds during the traditional haunting times, the hours of darkness.

But should you, dear reader, visit the Tower of London, do not get the impression that you are exempt from similar experiences; do not think for one minute that the Past will not reach out and tap you on the shoulder, to remind you of the horrors and violence enacted within this most historic of castles.

Within and around the towers the memories linger, waiting perhaps to reveal themselves to those whose thoughts or sympathies may be receptive to them.

A candle flame is almost invisible in the sunlight – but it is still there. So it is with the Ghosts of the Tower of London – and if you look where the shadows linger, in the corners, round the stairs – you may see them too.

Select Bibliography

Tower of London	W G Bell	1920
The Beauchamp Tower	W R Dick	1863
Her Majesty's Tower	Hepworth Dixon	1885
Tower of London	R Davey	1910
Memoirs of the Tower of London	Britton and Brayley	1830
History of the Tower	J Bayley	1830
Tower of London from Within	G Younghusband	1919
Walks in London	A J C Hare	1878
Romance of London	J Timbs	1865
Old and New London (magazines)		1874